GARDENER'S MANUAL;

CONTAINING

PLAIN INSTRUCTIONS FOR THE SELECTION, PREPARATION, AND

MANAGEMENT OF A

KITCHEN GARDEN:

WITH PRACTICAL DIRECTIONS FOR THE CULTI-
VATION AND MANAGEMENT OF SOME

OF THE MOST USEFUL

CULINARY VEGETABLES.

PUBLISHED BY THE UNITED SOCIETY,

New Lebanon, Columbia Co., N. Y.

Printed by

J. W. KELLEY,

424 BROADWAY, NEW-YORK.

1843.

PRICE SIX CENTS.

To Gardeners,

AND

DEALERS IN GARDEN SEEDS.

The design of this little Manual is to enable our trading customers, while furnishing their assortment of Garden Seeds, to afford instructions, at a trifling expense, to such of their customers as may wish to obtain some practical information relative to the raising and management of those valuable kitchen vegetables, which are considered the most useful and important in a family.

Having had many years' experience in raising seeds and vegetables, and in proving the quality of seeds,—and we are not ignorant of the complaints which are often made of bad seeds,—we are fully convinced that good seeds are sometimes condemned for want of a fair trial, and especially for the want of a seasonable and right management in preparing the ground and putting in the seed. We know full well the loss and perplexity of sowing poor seeds, and the reasonable anxiety of those who purchase for sale, to procure such seeds as will satisfy their customers : and yet the venders are sometimes blamed and charged with imposing on their customers, in consequence of the failure of their seeds, when the fault is altogether owing to the want of proper management in the gardeners. We have therefore endeavored to furnish a small and convenient Manual, which we trust will prove beneficial to all who deal in Garden seeds, and more especially to those who have had but little experience in cultivating a kitchen garden, by furnishing such plain and practical directions as are best calculated to ensure success.

Our original stock of Garden seeds have been carefully selected, with a view to obtain those that are most useful, from the numerous varieties cultivated in the country, and those we offer for sale are raised under our own immediate care and direction, excepting a few kinds which cannot be raised to perfection in this climate : also when we have a failure in some particular kinds of seed, (which sometimes happens,) in order to supply the deficiency, and accommodate our customers, we purchase of credible Seeds-men, and test their vitality before offering them for sale—we can therefore recommend them to be pure and genuine.

Note.—The time for planting and sowing seeds, as directed in the following pages, is calculated as a medium for the vicinity of Albany, or about 42 deg. N. Latitude, and by observing the different degrees of heat and cold throughout the country, the proper time for putting in seed will be found to vary from 30 to 60 days or more, being earlier to the south and later to the north—therefore it becomes necessary for the gardener to notice the climate, season, situation of the soil, &c., to apply these directions to profit.

INTRODUCTION.

Many books have been written upon the subject of gardening, and ingenious authors have suggested various means for improving and embellishing them, that the common classes, those to whom a garden is of the most real value, cannot hope to attain for several ages, if ever.

The manners of cultivation recommended by some, are expensive in a corresponding degree, well calculated for lords and nobles, who can afford a tenant to every square acre, but quite impracticable by those who have to tend their own gardens and conduct a farm, or some mechanical profession besides, which is the case with the majority of garden-holders in this country : and it is such that this little sketch is designed to benefit. These pages contain no suggestion or instruction, but what may be made practical to almost every farmer in the United States.

The present condition of the majority of gardens in this country, is susceptible of much improvement, which the spirit of the age, and the progressive improvements in agriculture, loudly demand.—Many are unfavorably situated, and not large enough ; many are of ill shape, and not well laid out internally. Very many are deficient in the variety of vegetables cultivated ; and a majority not properly prepared before stocking with seeds and plants, and but poorly cultivated when stocked. These things should not be ; the garden is said to be an index of the owners mind. If this be true, many who otherwise might be acquitted, must be judged to possess minds susceptible of much improvement in order, usefulness, and beauty. But a claim, as strong perhaps, as any that may be urged for the improvement of the kitchen garden, is its usefulness, and the superiority of a well cultivated garden, over the poor neglected patch. That a garden is very necessary and useful, almost every body admits, by trying to have something of the kind; but that a well prepared and a well cultivated one, is as much superior to a neglected one, as it really is, doubtless many who love idleness, even better than they love themselves, will be slow to admit; but experience has proved that the crop will be improved by good cultivation, both in quantity and quality, more than in proportion to the additional expense incurred, till perfection is attained, where, of course, improvement must stop.

It has been the aim, in this work, to be brief and comprehensive, to compress much into little space; therefore such general directions as apply to many or all varieties of vegetables, are given in chapters by themselves, which prevents the necessity of repeating them under every several vegetable, to which they may apply. By reading the book through, it is believed, all the information necessary for the management of a Kitchen Garden, and cultivation of the most useful culinary vegetables may be obtained.

The Publishers.

New Lebanon, April 20, 1843.

THE GARDENER'S MANUAL

CHAPTER I.

DIRECTIONS FOR THE SELECTION OF A GARDEN SPOT AND IMPLEMENTS.

As some of our readers may not, as yet, have selected a garden spot, nor obtained the implements requisite for prosecuting the business of gardening, a few remarks upon the situation, soil, size, and implements necessary, may not be improper.

1. *Situation.*—In choosing a site for a garden, a spot of even land, slightly inclining to the south or east, and having the full benefit of the sun, is to be preferred. It should be situated near the dwelling, and neatly enclosed with a high wall, or a tight board fence.

2. *Soil.*—Deep, dry, light, and rich, are the essential requisites of a good garden soil; and if not so naturally, it should be made so by art. If wet, draining should be resorted to; if too shallow, deep ploughing; if poor, manuring; if stony, they should be got off:—and thus should every impediment and obstruction to a good sweet soil, be reversed or removed, by industry and art.

3. *Size.*—The size of a garden depends upon the number to be supplied from it, and the kinds of vegetables intended to be raised in it. For a family of six persons, one quarter of an acre is sufficient for most of the kinds raised from seeds commonly retailed at the country stores. But if desirable to have fruit trees, shrubs, strawberry beds, early potatoes, &c., enclosed within the same fence that encloses the garden, it must be made larger, in proportion to the quantity wanted.

The *shape* of the garden should be either square or oblong, both for convenience and looks.

4. *Implements.*—These are a plough, harrow, rake, hoes, spade, shovel, dung-fork, watering pot, transplanting-trowel, a long and strong line, or cord, and a wooden roller 18 inches in diameter and 4 feet long. Perhaps bean poles, pea brush, a quantity of garden stakes and twine, might with propriety be added to the list. These are generally sufficient, if the directions under the article *Soil*, have been previously and properly attended to, although we are aware that others will at times be wanted, as the crow-bar in setting bean poles, the pruning knife, shears, or sickle in trimming and gathering the crops at times, &c., &c.

CHAPTER II.

OF PREPARING THE GROUND, AND PUTTING IN CROPS.

Considering the garden as fenced, drained, and cleared of stones, if neccessary,the next consideration is the preparation of the ground for the reception of seeds and plants. As gardening should not be undertaken on turf land just broken up, we shall consider the garden free from turf, and considerably ameliorated, as it should be, by a crop of potatoes, or other roots, previously to using it for the rarer kinds of vegetables. In this state, let it be manured, in quantity and quality, according to the previous richness of the soil.— And here let it be stated, once for all, that all culinary vegetables do best upon a good rich soil; therefore let your land, if not naturally quite rich, be plentifully manured; and even if the land be quite fertile, if it has been used much, a slight manuring will be beneficial. Poor land should be manured at the rate of 40 ox cart loads per acre; on good land less will suffice.

The best manure for a garden is a compost, of one part mineral substances, as ashes, lime, sand or clay, (as the soil may require,) salt, &c.: five parts vegetable matter, as weeds, straw, leaves, roots and stalks of plants, and tan bark or sawdust to make the soil light, if necessary: and six parts of animal excrement. These should be collected in the course of the season, and mixed well together, to cause them to ferment. In the fall, this compost should be spread evenly upon the garden, and ploughed in, that it may be ready for action as soon as the state of the ground will allow, in the Spring, without having to wait for an operation that may much better be performed in the Fall.

Considering the garden as having been well manured in the Fall, or early in the Spring, the next thing is to plough it, which should not be done till quite dry; for ploughing it when wet in the Spring, will cause it to be much more lumpy, and harder through the whole season, than it would be if suffered to get thoroughly dry before ploughing. Deep ploughing is the only kind wanted in preparing a garden, the deeper the better in most soils. Next comes the harrow; this should do its work faithfully, when a second and last ploughing, dividing the garden into beds, should be resorted to.— To effect this, strike a furrow through the middle of the spot where you wish to have your bed, go back on the other side close by the furrow just made, turning the earth against that thrown out from the first furrow, and so continue going round your bed, (which is thus begun,) and turning the earth towards the centre, till it is as wide as desirable; then proceed to make the others in the same way, till the garden is all made into beds or plats, in size and width suited to the kinds and quantities of vegetables to be grown on them. This plan of ploughing and forming beds, will leave little hollows or ditches between them, which should be kept open to drain off the superabundant water in wet weather.

The next thing is to rake the beds ; which, on those designed for fine seeds or those to be sown in drills, should be thoroughly and finely done. On those designed for planting beans, squashes, &c., you need not be so particular.

Sowing.—Stretch a line from end to end, over your bed, for a guide in drilling, then with the corner of your hoe, a pointed stick, or an instrument made for the purpose, drill shallow furrows across the bed from north to south, in depth and distance apart, accommodated to the kinds of seeds you wish to sow, according to directions given hereafter, under the names of the respective plants.

Fall Sowing.—Some seeds may be sown in the Fall, with success ; and the plants will be up considerable earlier next Spring, in consequence. But as Fall sowing is attended with considerable risk, and extra labor, it should be generally avoided, except for such seeds as vegetate very slowly, and will be greatly forwarded by the action of the frost, without the risk of losing the seed by premature vegetation. Perhaps Asparagus, and Sea Kale, are the only kinds of this description, in our catalogue. For Fall sowing, the ground should be prepared as directed for Spring sowing, and the various seeds put in just so late as that they will not sprout before the Winter sets in, for sprouting will spoil them. As soon as the frost has fairly closed the ground, the beds should be covered a foot deep with litter, straw, or boughs of ever-green, to prevent the frost from penetrating too deeply ; these should be removed early in the Spring, and you will have the plants quickly up.

Ridging.—Some gardeners sow and plant many kinds of seeds upon ridges. For some seeds, especially in low flat land, this is a good practice. Have your ground well prepared, as directed for the garden, throw two furrows together with a large plough, for one ridge, level and pulverize with a rake, and it is prepared for sowing or planting.

Soaking Seeds.—In a very dry season, or when you happen to be very late in stocking your garden. soaking the seed a few hours, in luke-warm water, will be beneficial to some kinds ; but generally, if sown in proper season, all good seeds will germinate quite as well without soaking, and to seeds of the cabbage kind, it is a positive injury.

Planting.—This term applies to putting seeds in bunches or hills, the distance between which must be accommodated to the kind of vegetable to be raised. Stretch the line as directed for sowing, but instead of drilling make hills, or slight elevations of the soil, a foot in diameter and three inches high, with a southern in-

clination. In a dry season, the earth should always be pressed upon the top of the seeds. On level beds, it may be done with a roller ; on seeds planted in hills, with the back of the hoe.

Transplanting.—This is an important part of the gardeners business, and to perform it successfully is very desirable.

A prevalent, but erroneous opinion concerning transplanting is,
that it should be done just before a shower, in order to succeed
well ; but experience has shown that a day or two after, when the
ground has become dry enough to work again, in the evening, is a
preferable time, and perhaps, with the exception of cloudy weather,
is the best that can be selected. The ground should be prepared as
directed for sowing, the plants should be taken up with as much
dirt as possible adhering to them, which will be promoted by watering plentifully, before taking them up. A hole deep enough for
the roots to enter at full length, should be made, the plants set up-
right, and fine fresh earth gently pressed against the roots on all
sides. Tender plants will sometimes need watering and shading a
day or two after transplanting.

CHAPTER III.

OF CULTIVATION.

Hoeing, is usually the first act of cultivation in the garden
which should be performed as soon as the plants are fairly up, and
continued as often as neccessary, for destroying weeds or nourish-
ing the plants through the season, with punctuality and faithfulness.

There are three manners of hoeing necessary to be made use of
in the garden, which may be distinguished by the names of 1st.
flat hoeing, 2nd., digging, and 3d., hilling. The first is made use
of merely to kill the weeds ; the second to promote the growth of
the plants, by mellowing the soil, and the third to support and nou-
rish some plants in their more advanced stages, by drawing the earth
up around their stems, or stalks.

Weeding should be early performed, and continued with perseve-
ring faithfulness, as often as necessary, through the season.

Thinning may be performed at twice, the first time as soon as
the plants are fairly in sight, the second after they are large enough
to show which will make thrifty plants. As the quality of the crop,
as well as the quantity, frequently depends very much upon this
branch of cultivation, it is important that it be seasonably and faithfully performed. Leaving plants too thick is a prevalent error, and
one to which gardeners are very liable.

Ploughing.—Where there is room for a single horse plough, or horse hoe, to run between the rows, without injury, it should be improved, as it will save much time and labor, and be highly beneficial to the plants.

Watering.—Some gardeners spend much useless labor in sprinkling water over and around their plants. When the ground is very dry, at the time you wish to transplant, watering the ground where you intend to set the plants, a day or two beforehand, may be beneficial : watering hot beds is also necessary and indispensable. But to plants in open ground, that have good roots, watering in the customary way, with a hand watering pot, is of but little use. If you have a stream of running water at your command, which can be turned upon your garden, something more effectual may be performed. But in default of this, digging and stirring the soil should be resorted to, which will cause the moisture below the surface, (the *life and dependance of plants in a dry time,*) to rise freely.

Bleaching.—This is an operation for whitening the leaves of some salad vegetables. With some, it is performed by tying up the outside leaves, so as to exclude the light from those within ;— with others, by hilling them up with earth, as they advance in growth.

CHAPTER IV.

DIRECTIONS FOR MAKING AND MANAGING A HOT-BED.

Such vegetables as are wanted for early use, or such as require the whole season to bring them to maturity, may be brought forward nearly a month earlier, by being sown early in a hot-bed, and transplanted in the open ground, when the weather has become mild and the soil prepared for vegetation. The hot-bed should always be located on the south side of a building, or a high wall.— The frame to receive the sashes should be four feet wide, and as long as you desire, the inclination to the south will be about right if the back of the frame is 18 inches high to have the front 9 inches. To this frame, let the sashes be nicely fitted, to exclude rats, mice, and cold weather.

Having prepared the frame, find its dimensions, and mark out the spot for building the bed 6 inches larger every way, than the frame ; drive down a stake at each corner as a guide in building the bed. For this, the best material is unfermented horse dung, with the litter or straw among it, as it usually comes from the stable. In taking from a heap of this, get the inside as well as the out, both long and short, and mix them well together. If the litter be not in the proportion of one half or more, increase it by adding fresh straw. Take this to the spot where you are to make your bed, put it on, a forkful at a time, shaking it well to pieces, spreading it evenly, and beating it well down as you proceed, particularly the edges. Raise it to the height of 4 feet, then put on the frame, and let it stand till the heat rises.

Now put within the frame, on the top of the dung, 8 inches in depth, of light, rich soil, then cover all up, and let it stand a week or more, till the earth is well warmed, when it may be sown. Make the drills from north to south, and 3 inches apart, in depth according to the kind of seeds sown.

From this time the bed must be watched and attended with particular care. Every morning, as soon as the sun is fairly up, the glasses should be raised a little, to admit fresh air; and in a warm day they may be entirely removed. If the glasses are left on, under a hot sun, without the admission of air, more than two hours, the plants will be scalded by the steam thus excited within the bed. More failures arise in hot-bed culture, from want of air, than from all other causes combined.

Watering is a very essential part of the hot-bed management; it should be done in the morning, with a fine sprinkler, and with water of the temperature of rain in Summer. The earth should be often mellowed among the plants, to admit the water freely, and promote their growth; weeds should be uprooted, and the suggestions concerning thinning, heretofore given, should, of all places, in the hot-bed, be most punctually attended to; as a rule, a plant in the hot-bed should be as distant from another plant, as its top or longest shoot is from its own root.

Many regard hot-beds as more expensive than profitable : but this is an error, they are not expensive property ; it is true their management is quite particular, and requires you to be thoughtful and regular ; but this is only promoting a good habit, and if you were inclined to forgetfulness, would almost justify keeping one expressly for that purpose. In a large garden a good hot-bed will more than pay for itself, annually, and in any garden, worthy of the name, the benefits are double the expense.

CHAPTER V.

OF INSECTS INJURIOUS TO THE GARDENER.

Cutworms, root-worms, slugs or snails, cabbage-lice, turnip-flies, and yellow bugs, are the insects that most trouble the kitchen gardener.

Cut-worm.—This insect commits its depredations in the night ; and immediately, on the appearance of day light, secretes itself under the dirt, near the plant which it last attacked ; consequently there it may be found and easily destroyed which perhaps is the most effectual and only sure method of killing them. They prey upon Beans, Corn, Peppers, Onions, Radishes, and Cabbage plants, in their infant state, cutting off the leaves and sometimes the stems or stalks,

Root-worm.—These attack the roots of all plants, of the cabbage kind, those of melons and cucumbers, and are well known to be especially fond of turnips and radishes. To prevent their depredations, pour old fermented urine, salt water, or weak lye, directly around the roots, or what is the same in effect, scatter around a little salt, or wood ashes. As a preventative, which is ever preferable to a cure, never put these vegetables on the same ground they occupied the previous year.

Slugs or shelless snails, may be destroyed by strewing ashes or quick lime over them.

Cabbage-lice.—These always infest the weakest, poorest plants; therefore those who have the most good thrifty plants will suffer least. But as in some instances, extirpation is the only means of saving an entire crop from ruin, we would advise always to begin the work in season, before the lice become so numerous as to render it an impracticable undertaking.

Plaster, ashes, or quick lime, sprinkled over them in a dewy morning will check their progress; but will not destroy them, unless rubbed in. To effect this, a brush or cloth may be used, unfolding the leave with one hand and applying the brush with the other. A decoction of tobacco, administered with a sponge in the same way, is very effectual ; fermented urine is equally so.

Turnip-fly or Garden-flea.—This insect attacks plants in their infant state, feasting upon their tender leaves to the great annoyance of the gardener and destruction of the plants. Melons, Cucumbers, Squashes, Cabbages, and Turnips, are their favorite food. Covering the plants with chaff, fine shavings, or sawdust, till they are out of danger, we have found to be the most effectual mode of preventing their ravages.

When this cannot be afforded, snuff, soot, or sulphur finely pulverised, and sprinkled over and under the plants while wet with dew, is beneficial. But as plants are subject to material injury from these insects, only while in an infant state, the chief aim should be to have the land so prepared, seeded, and cultivated, as to give the plants a vigorous, thrifty growth, which will soon place them out of danger.

Yellow or striped bugs.—Another enemy of the Cucumber tribe. Its depredations may be essentially checked by sprinkling the plants when wet, with a composition of Rye-flour, Ashes and Plaster, having equal quantities of each, thoroughly mixed. Water saturated with cow-dung, is also said to be a good remedy.

To be sure of a crop, as all means of preventing the ravages of insects may at times fail, it is well to put in plenty of the seed of such plants as are attacked by them, which with the precautions heretofore given, to take means for having thrifty plants, is, in many instances, the only means of ensuring a crop.

CHAPTER VI.

A Catalogue of Garden Seeds

RAISED AND PUT UP BY THE UNITED SOCIETY OF SHAKERS,

NEW LEBANON, COLUMBIA CO., N. Y.

Asparagus, Giant
Bean, Early China, (bush)
"   "   Purple   "
"   "   White   "
"   Royal White   "
"   Clapboard, (pole)
"   Cranberry   "
Beet, Early Scarcity.
"   "   Turnip
"   Yellow Sugar
"   White French do.
"   Long Blood
"   Mangel Wurtzel
Cabbage, Early York
"   "   Sugar Loaf
"   Large Drumhead
"   Green Savoy
"   Red Dutch
Cauliflower, Early
Carrot, Long Orange
"   Early Horn
"   Altringham
Celery, White
Corn, Early Canada
"   Sweet or Sugar
Cucumber, Early Frame
"   "   Cluster
"   Extra Long
"   Long Green
Egg Plant

Lettuce, Early Imperial
"   "   Curled
"   "   Dutch
"   Ice Coss
"   Cabbage-head
"   Frankfort   "
Melon, Large Water
"   Long Musk
"   Nutmeg   "
Nasturtium
Onion, White Portugal
"   Yellow Dutch
"   Large Red
Parsley, Curled or Double
Parsnip, Long White
Peas, Early Washington
"   "   Frame
"   Large Marrowfat
"   Tall Sugar
Pepper, Squash
"   Sweet
"   Large Bell
Pepper Grass, Double
Radish, Short Top Scarlet
"   Scarlet Turnip
"   Long Salmon
"   Black Winter
"   Large Dutch
Rhubarb
Saffron, American.

Sage, English	Squash, Winter Crookneck
Salsify, or Vegetable Oyster	" Summer "
Savory, Summer	Tomato, Large Red
Sea Kale	Turnip, Early Flat
Spinage, Roundleaf	" Flat Field
Squash, Sweet Potato	". Long Tankared
" Summer Scollop	" Ruta Baga

CHAPTER VII.

PARTICULAR TREATMENT
OF THE DIFFERENT VARIETIES OF CULINARY VEGETABLES.

Asparagus.—*F. Asperge.*—*S. Esparrago.**—This is a very delicious esculent vegetable, and easily cultivated, after the first operation of preparing the ground. It is sown the first year, and transplanted the second.

First Year.—Sow as soon as the ground can be prepared in the Spring, in drills 18 inches apart, and 2 inches deep. It is three or four weeks in coming up, and should therefore be sown on land free from the seed of weeds, lest the weeds come up first; greatly to the injury of the young plants. Thin to 8 inches distance between the plants in the row.

Second Year.—Prepare your bed by working a bountiful supply of strong manure into the ground, to the depth of 18 inches. Level the top of the bed, stretch your line, and with a hoe, shovel, or plough, mark out drills 6 inches deep, and 2 feet apart. In these drills, or rather furrows, set the asparagus roots of last years' growth, 20 inches asunder ; these roots will spread, and in a few years, asparagus will shoot up in every part of the bed.

When the setting out is completed, level the top of the bed and let it grow up. Every succeeding Spring the stalks should be cut up, and hauled off or burned on the ground. The buds or young shoots, which is the part used, will be fit for cutting the third year ; they should be cut sparingly the first year, but thereafter, the cutting may be continued until the first of July, when a coat of dung should be spread on and turned under, and the asparagus suffered to run up to seed.

Kidney Beans.—*F. Feve.*—*S. Haba.*—These are delicate plants, and the seed should not be hurried into the ground till it is well dried and warmed by the sun. The first of May is

---

* The French and Spanish names of the various vegetables are added to our common English name, and marked with the letters F, and S., for the information of foreigners who purchase our seeds.

14

soon enough in this lattitude. (Albany.) The dwarf or bush beans may be sown in drills, 20 inches apart, 2 inches deep, and 6 inches apart in the row.

The *Running* or *Pole Beans* should be planted in hills, three and a half feet distant each way. We prefer setting the poles before planting. For this purpose we stretch a line, and set the poles by it; then dig and loosen the earth, and drop five or six beans in a circle round the pole, about 3 inches from it, and cover with mellow dirt one inch or one and a half in depth.— When the plants are well up, stir the earth around them, and pull out the weakest plants, leaving three to each hill. This should be done when they are perfectly dry; for beans never should be hoed when wet, nor when any dew is on them.

The green pods of beans may be kept and preserved fresh by laying them down in a jar or tub, with a layer of salt between each layer of beans.

Beet.—F. Betterave.—S. Beterraga—Sow very early, in drills 18 inches apart, and 1 deep. Thin the first time to 4 inches, the last to 8.

Cabbage.—F. Chou.—S. Col.—For an early crop, a quantity may be sown in the hot-bed the 10th of April, and transplanted out the 10th of May, which will be the proper time for sowing the general crop. Sow in small beds, each kind by itself; sow early and late at the same time, thereby to ensure a constant succession of heads; the early furnishing a supply for Fall use, and the late holding out even till the ensuing Spring. As soon as fairly up, thin to 4 inches distance, each way; let them stand here till they have 6 leaves, then transplant.

The early kinds, being small, will do at 2 feet apart each way, the late large kinds should have three and a half or four feet.— Digging or ploughing between them occasionally, will be highly beneficial.

Cauliflower.—F. Choufleur.—S. Coliflor.—At the south they are sown in hot-beds in the Fall, and protected through the Winter; but in this climate, they should be sown in the hot-bed early in the Spring. In about three weeks they should be transplanted into a bed of lower temperature, and by the middle of May, again transplanted into the garden.

Carrot.—F. Carotte.—S. Zanahoria.—Sow the same as beets, and thin to 4 inches.

Celery.—F. Celeri.—S. Apio.—This is an excellent salad vegetable, and is prepared for the table by bleaching. It should be sown in the hot-bed by the 10th of April. It vegetates slowly, but surely; if your seed is good, and properly put in and attended. When the plants are six inches high, they should be taken from the hot-bed and set into mellow ground, 4 inches distant each way, to remain till your early peas, or some other early beds are cleared off, and then put into trenches upon the same ground. Lay out your trenches about 18 inches wide, allowing six feet space between each trench; plough or spade out the earth from the trenches to the depth of sixteen or eighteen inches, if the depth of soil will admit; put about three inches of very rotten manure into the trench; then throw in upon this manure about five inches of the best soil; mix and stir the manure and soil well together; then set your plants by a line in the centre of the trench, leaving a space of six or eight inches between them. Pull off all the suckers or side shoots before setting.

When they have attained the height of ten inches, you may commence earthing them up; but never do it while the plants are wet. In performing this, care should be taken to gather all the leaves up with the hand while drawing the earth up equally on each side of the row, being careful to leave the hearts of the plants open. Repeat the earthing once a week or oftener, till about the last week in October. From this time it will not grow much, but it is better to let it stand out till the ground is about to be locked up by frost, then dig it and pack it away in the cellar. It will keep till May.

———

Corn.—F. Mais.—S. Maiz.—The Early Canada is the earliest kind of corn we raise, and is preferred only for being several weeks earlier than the common field corn. The Sweet or Sugar Corn is best for cooking in its green state, as it remains much longer in the milk, and is richer and sweeter than any other kind. It is rather later than the common field corn, and is therefore fit for the table when the field corn has become too hard.

This corn may be preserved for winter use, by parboiling it when green, and cutting it from the cob and drying it in the sun. It then affords a wholesome and agreeable dish when cooked like bean porridge, or what is called *succotash.*

Plant the 20th of May, in hills 4 feet distant each way. Cultivate the same as other corn, by ploughing, hilling, &c.

———

Cucumber.—F. Concomber.—S. Cohambro.—The 20th of May

is soon enough to plant cucumbers here. Hills to be 4 feet distant each way. One plant is enough for a hill, ultimately; but to make provision for insects, plenty of seed should be put in, and the plants afterwards thinned out.

Egg Plant.—F. Malongene.—S. Sechugar.—Sow the seeds in March, in a hot bed, and plant them out towards the latter part of May, in a rich, warm piece of ground, in rows 3 feet apart, and at the distance of two feet in the rows. They bear their fruit when about a foot high, which if rightly prepared, is by many esteemed equal to eggs. Some are very fond of them when sliced and fried with ham.

Lettuce.—F. Laitue.—S. Lachuga.—Sow as early as possible in the Spring, and at intervals through the season, in drills 1 foot apart and ½ an inch deep. The early kinds need but little thinning; but head Lettuce should stand 8 or 10 inches apart, or they will have but inferior heads, and if very thick, none at all.

Melon.—F. and S. the same.—Musk melons require the same treatment as cucumbers. Watermelons should be planted further apart. A shovel full of ashes applied to each hill and mixed with the soil is beneficial.

Nasturtium.—F. Capucine.—S. Nasturcio.—This is an annual plant, a native of Peru, and is much cultivated for the berries, which if gathered while green and pickled in vinegar, make a good substitute for capers. Sow as early as the season will admit, in drills an inch deep. The plants should be supported from the ground by bushy sticks, or otherwise, in order to have them do well and produce a plentiful crop of good fruit.

Onion.—F. Oignon.—S. Cebolla.—Sow early in drills, 16 inches apart and half an inch deep. Thin to 4 or 6 inches.
  The onions will be ripe in September. When the tops are sufficiently dry, pull the onions, and let them lie a few days in the sun to dry; then gather them up and house them.

Parsley.—F. Persil.—S. Peregil.—A salutary pot herb. Cultivate the same as early Lettuce.

Parsnip.—F. Panais.—S. Pastinaca.—Cultivate as Carrots. In November dig enough for winter use, and put in the cellar; let the rest stand in the ground till spring.

Peas.—F. Pois.—S. Guisante.—The late and tall kinds should be sown in double drills 4 or 5 feet apart, and supported with brush. The early kinds may be sown on ridges at 3 feet distance and a foot high. This will form trenches which will carry off the water and should be kept open at the lower end. When the peas are off, every alternate trench may be prepared for celery.

If your seed peas contain bugs, we would recommend to scald them by putting them into a tub or pail, and pouring in boiling water enough to cover them , and stirring them briskly about a minute ; then pour off the water and add a little cold water to them and sow them soon. This will destroy the bugs without injuring the peas.

Pepper.—F. Piment.—S. Pimiento.—These should be sown in the hot bed in April, and transplanted out the first of June, 2 feet distant each way.

Pepper grass, or Curled Cress.—F. Cresson.—S. Berros.—An agreeable salad, cultivate as early Lettuce.

Radish.—F. Rave.—S. Nabe.—Sow and cultivate the same as onions. As they soon become too old for the table, they should be sown once a fortnight, in order to have a supply through the season.

Rhubarb, or Pie Plant.—Rheum Undulatum.—Sow the first year very early in drills, 2 feet apart and an inch in depth. Thin to 10 inches. The second year transplant them out 4 feet distant each way. Shade them from the hot sun, both the first and second year, till they gain good roots. The seed stalks should not be suffered to grow. The stalks or stems of the leaves, cut up and prepared, are as good for pies as currants or goose berries, and six, weeks earlier. The roots are used in medicine.

Saffron.—F. Saffran.—S. Azafran.—A medicinal herb: the flowers are the part used. Sow in double drills 3 feet apart ; thin to 6 inches.

Sage.—F. Sauge.—S. Salvia.—Sow in drills 2 feet apart, and thin to 8 or 10 inches in the row. It is a perennial ; but as young plants produce the best leaves, it should be resown once in 2 years.

Salsify or Vegetable oyster.—F. Salsifis.—S. Salsifi.—This vegetable, in appearance, resembles a small parsnip ; it is raised annually from the seed, and may be cultivated in the same manner as parsnips or carrots, and is as easily raised.

It is a vegetable highly esteemed by those best acquainted with it. It is very hardy, and may stand in the ground through the winter, if you wish.

Savory Summer.—F. Sariette de l'ete.—Sow in shallow drills one foot apart in April or May, Summer Savory tea is a good remedy for the nervous head ache, drink it hot just before going to bed.

Sea Kale.—F. Choud' Econsse.—This is a capital article ; the cultivation and use are the same as those of Asparagus.　　Break the shells before sowing.

Squash.—F. Giraumon.---S. Especie de la Calabaza.---Squashes require to be treated much after the manner of melons and cucumbers.　The Sweet Potato Squash and *Winter Crook-neck,* as they produce running vines, require to be planted in hills at the distance of six or eight feet. The *Summer Crook-neck* and the *Summer-Scollop,* being what are called *bush Squashes,* as they have no running vines, may be planted in hills about four feet apart each way.

Tomato or Love Apple.—F. Tomate.—S. Tomatera.—This is a very healthy vegetable, and a great favorite when we become accustomed to it, though generally not very palatable at first. They should be sown in the hot-bed in April, and when the ground becomes warm, and the danger from frost is over, they may be transplanted out, 4 or 5 feet distant each way.　The fruit will ripen better if the vines are supported by a trellis, or something similar, to elevate them from the ground a little.

Turnip.—F. Navet.---S. Nabo.—Sow and cultivate the same as Onions, in the Garden.　See *Field Culture,* next chapter.

CHAPTER VIII.

FIELD CULTURE OF GARDEN VEGETABLES.

Beets, Carrots. Parsnips, Rutabaga Turnips, Flat Turnips, and Peas, are sometimes raised in the field for cattle or swine. For the first four, a spot occupied with potatoes the previous year, should be chosen ; this should be prepared as directed for preparing the garden ; and for Carrots and Parsnips, the cultivation is the same as in the garden ; but Beets and Rutabagas should be sown on slightly elevated ridges, at the distance of three feet, to admit of ploughing between them. Rutabagas should be sown about the 10th of June.

For Flat Turnips and Peas, a spot of turf land should be broken up in the Fall. The next season, before sowing, it should be bountifully manured, and thoroughly ploughed and harrowed; sow the seed broadcast, and harrow it in. Peas should be sown in April or May, and much thicker than many farmers sow them. Turnips for Winter use, should be sown about the middle or last of July, with a sparing hand.

Eight pounds of beet seed are sufficient to sow an acre, as above directed; 4 lbs of Carrot or Parsnip seed; 2 lbs of Rutabaga, and 1 lb of flat Turnip. Peas should be sown at the rate of two and a half, or three bushels to the acre, according to the strength of soil and kind of peas.

CHAPTER IX.

PRESERVATION OF VEGETABLES IN WINTER.

Beets and Carrots should be gathered before hard frosts in the Fall, the tops cut off and the roots packed away in sand in a warm cellar. A good method of preserving Beets and Carrots fresh through the Winter is, to lay them in a circular form on the bottom of the cellar, with the roots in the centre and heads outward; cover the first course of roots with sand; then lay another course upon them, and cover with sand as before, and so on until all are packed and covered. The sand for Carrots should be very dry or they will rot; for Beets it may be moist, but not wet. Celery is preserved in the same way. Onions and Turnips keep well on scaffolds, or in barrels, in a dry cool cellar.

To preserve Cabbages.—Freezing does not hurt Cabbages, provided you can keep them frozen; repeated thawing is what does the mischief. Therefore make a ridge 2 feet high, 6 feet wide, and as long as you need, on the north side of a building; on this lay some poles crosswise, and on the poles some narrow boards lengthwise, 2 inches apart. Take up your Cabbages in a dry day, just before Winter, strip off some of the outside leaves, and set them, roots upward, on the boards, cover them a foot deep with straw or corn stalks, and they will keep fresh and green.

To preserve Sweet, Pot, and Medicinal herbs and flowers, they should be gathered when in bloom, thoroughly dried and put up in tight boxes or jars, till wanted for use.

CHAPTER X.

OF THE USES OF VEGETABLES.

Under this head the vegetables of the garden may be divided into 4 classes, 1st., those of which we use the root, 2nd., the herbage, 3d., the fruit, 4th the flower.

1st *Roots*—Beets, Carrots, Onions, Parsnips, Radishes, Salsify, and Turnips, are the vegetables of which the roots are used. That all these, in one shape or another, are consumed by man, is supposed to be generally understood ; but how many and which can be most profitably fed to cattle or other stock, every reader may not know.

Beets are highly and justly recommended for feeding milch cows in the fall and winter, and especially in the Spring, if well preserved ; also, for fattening beef and pork. If fed in the raw state, they should be cut fine ; if boiled, a little Indian meal or bran may be mixed with them.

Carrots are excellent for fattening beef, and for milch cows. Horses are remarkably fond of them. When cut up small, and mixed with cut straw and given them, with a little hay, it is said they may be kept in excellent condition for any kind of ordinary labor, without any grain.

Milch cows should be fed sparingly with beets and carrots at first, or they will incline to fatten, to the injury of their milking properties.

Parsnips are excellent food for neat cattle, sheep, hogs or horses. Beef fatted on parsnips, is said to command a higher price in England, than fatted in any other way. Milch cows fed on parsnips, are said to give richer milk, and yield more butter, than from any other food. Hogs are also said to fatten very easily on them, and to produce superior pork. Cattle are sometimes averse to parsnips at first, but they will soon learn to relish them, after which they will eat them with avidity.

Turnips are excellent for sheep ; Rutabaga turnips are also good for cattle ; they should be cut up fine and mixed with Indian meal.

2. *Herbage.*—Asparagus, Cabbage, Celery, Lettuce, Parsely, Peppergrass, Rhubarb, Sage, Savory, Spinnage and Sea Kale, are the main vegetables raised for their herbage, although the tops and leaves of others are frequently used. Cabbage leaves, and heads, are excellent for cattle, especially late in the fall, when grass has become scarce ; also the tops of beets, carrots and turnips, which may be safely taken off at this time.

3. *Fruit*—Beans, Corn, Cucumbers, Melons, Peas, and Tomatoes,

are cultivated for their fruit. Beans are good for Sheep, with the pods and vines. Peas, ground up with rye or Indian corn, form a superior provender for fattening hogs.

4. *Flowers.*—Cauliflowers and Saffron. Perhaps the first of these might as properly be classed under herbage, as flowers, the part eaten being composed of stems and leaves, as well as flowers in miniature, the combination, from its form and appearance, being called a flower. The leaves are good for cattle ; the flowers, when properly cooked, are esteemed a luxury.

CHAPTER XI.

RECIPES FOR COOKERY, &C.

Directions for Cooking Asparagus.—Cut the buds when from three to six inches high. Take water enough to cover the stalks, and put in salt sufficient to season them well ; boil and skim the water, then put in the asparagus. Be careful to take them up as soon as they become tender, so as to preserve their true flavor and green color ; for boiling a little too long will destroy both. Serve up with melted butter or cream. Sea Kale may be cooked in the same way.

Salsify or Vegetable Oyster.—There are various modes of dressing and cooking this vegetable. It is very excellent boiled and mashed up like squash and turnip, with a little salt and butter.— Some make soup of it ; in that case it should be boiled and mashed fine, in order to increase the flavor of the soup ; a few pieces of salt codfish added, gives it a good relish. Others prefer it parboiled, and then sliced up and fried in batter, or without.

To Cook Cauliflower.—Cut it when close and white, and of a middling size ; cut the stem so as to separate the flower from the leaves below it. Let it lie in salt and water awhile ; then put it into boiling water, with a handful of salt. Keep the boiler uncovered, and skim the water well. A small flower will require about fifteen minutes boiling ; a large one, about twenty. Take it up as soon as a fork will easily enter the stem : a little longer boiling will spoil it. Serve it up with gravy or melted butter.

Sweet Potato Squash may be boiled and mashed up with butter, &c., as common squash, or cut into pieces and steamed, or baked, in which state it is, by many, considered equal to the Carolina Potato.

Tomatoes.—Take them when ripe and red, dip them into scald-

Note—It is generally important in vegetable cookery that the boiling be performed briskly, and with plenty of water.

ing water, and take off all the skin, cut in quarters and scrape out the seeds; then put them into a clean stew pan and let them simmer about fifteen minutes, then put in a little butter and pepper, stir them a few minutes and they are done. Some prefer adding some crumbs of wheat bread or grated crackers. For pies or preserves the tomato requires a little more sugar than the peach to make it equally palatable. The process of making is much the same as with other fruit. Tomatoes may be preserved fresh by covering them with sugar. The green fruit is often pickled, like the cucumber or pepper. When prepared according to the following directions they make an excellent sauce or gravy, for meat or fish :

Tomato Catchup, or Catsup.—Collect the fruit when fully ripe, before any frost appear, squeeze or bruise them well, and boil them slowly for half an hour, then strain them through a cloth, and put in salt, pepper and spices to suit the taste, then boil again and take off the scum that rises, so as to leave the liquor in its pure state—keep it boiling slowly until about one half of the juice is diminished, then let it cool and put it into clear glass bottles, corked tight and kept in a cool place for use. After standing awhile, should any sediment appear in the bottles, the liquor should be poured off into other bottles, and again corked tight.

Egg Plant.—"Cut into slices about a quarter of an inch thick, put them into a dish, and pour on boiling water, let them remain a minute or two ; drain off the water, and season with pepper and salt, or with thyme, marjoram, or summer savory, according to the palate to be suited ; dust them with flour and put them into a frying pan, which should be ready with hot beef drippings, or lard. When browned on one side, turn them and brown the other."

Sweet Peppers are commonly used, when fully ripe, as a salad ; or the core may be extracted and the cavity filled with mince meat, which, on being thus baked, receives a very agreeable relish.

Rhubarb.—Peel and wash one or two dozen sticks of Rhubarb : put them in a stew pan, with the peel of a lemon, a bit of cinnamon, two cloves, and as much moist sugar as will sweeten it; set it over a fire, and reduce it to a marmalade, pass it through a hair sieve ; then add the peel of a lemon and half a nutmeg grated, a quarter of a pound of good butter, and the yolks of 4 eggs and one white, and mix all well together: line a pie dish, that will just contain it, with a good puff paste, put the mixture in, and bake it half an hour."

Another.—"Prepare Rhubarb as above; cut it in small pieces into a tart-dish sweeten with loaf-sugar pounded : cover it over with a good short crust paste ; sift a little sugar over the top, and bake half an hour in a rather hot oven. Serve up cold."

To make sherbet from Rhubarb.—"Boil 6 or 8 sticks of Rhubarb ten minutes in a quart of water, strain the liquor through a tamis into a jug, with the peel of a lemon cut very thin, and two table-spoonfuls of clarified sugar, let it stand about 5 or 6 hours and it is fit to drink."

To cook Beans and Peas when ripe.—Soak them in cold water 12 hours ; then par boil them, and bake, or stew, with pork or saltpetre, sufficient to season and soften them. Beans generally require about 4 hours baking, and peas 3 hours.

CHAPTER XII.

PICKLING.

" *Nasturtium Berries* must be gathered when they have just attained their full size, and while they are green, plump, and tender. Spice the vinegar, and pour it on while hot."

Tomatoes.—" Select small sized fruit, let them lie three days in a salt pickle, drain them well, and to a half peck of Tomatoes, add half a pound best flour of mustard, one ounce black pepper, one half pound white mustard seed, a small quantity of horse-radish, one ounce of cloves, and half a dozen of white onions, sliced. No scalding is necessary, merely fill up the jars with cold wine vinegar."

Cucumbers.—These should always be cut from the vines, leaving a short stem upon the cucumber. Clean them and place them in a tub or jar. Prepare a brine very weak, and about as warm as you can bear your hand in, and put to them. Let this stand 24 hours or more : then pour it off ; scald and skim it well, adding a little more salt, and apply it to the pickles a little warmer than before. They may now stand 36 or 48 hours ; then draw off the brine, scald and recruit as before, making it still more salt and warmer than before. Let them stand in this 48 hours : then prepare a brine as strong as possible, boil and skim it well, and cool it.

Rinse your Cucumbers in cold water, and put them into this strong brine when cold. In this situation they will keep a year or more. Before eating, soak them in cold water 24 hours ; then sour with vinegar to suit the taste.

Another.—" Get cucumbers of about 4 inches long, and an inch in diameter. Put them into unglazed stone jars, and cover them with a brine of salt and water, made with a quarter of a pound of salt to a quart of water ; cover them down, and set them before the fire till they begin to turn yellow ; then pour off the water and cover them with hot vinegar ; set them again before the fire, and let them remain till they become green ; then pour off the vinegar, and have ready a pickle made of the strongest vinegar, to each quart of which put two ounces of black peppercorns, one of ginger, one of salt, half an ounce of allspice, half a drachm of cayenne, and about a quarter of an ounce of white mustard seed. Pour this in while hot, and fill up the jars two inches above the gherkins. Tie them up air tight with a piece of bladder dipped in the pickle, and leather. Open the jars in about a week, and fill them again with pickle."

Peppers.—Pick them while in a green state, and put them into a strong cold brine. Before eating, soak them in cold water 24 hours, and sour them at pleasure.

Beets.—Boil them, scrape off the skin, and soak them in vinegar 24 hours, or till wanted for use. When thus prepared they form an excellent substitute for pickled cucumbers.

Bean pods, when young and tender may be made very palatable by being firstly boiled, then soaked in vinegar a few hours; so also may many other kinds of vegetables.

Perhaps some who have long been acquainted with the foregoing recipes, or those which they consider preferable, may count their publication vain. For such they are not designed; but that they may prove beneficial to many, and an injury to none, is, our only intention and wish.